DEUTERONOMY

AT JOURNEY'S END

10 Publishing
a division of 10 of those.com

First published in Great Britain in 2016

British Library Cataloguing in Publication Data
A record for this book is available from the British Library

ISBN: 9781910587683
Designed by Diane Warnes
Printed in the UK

10Publishing, a division of 10ofthose.com
Unit C, Tomlinson Road, Leyland, PR25 2DY, England
Email: info@10ofthose.com
Website: www.10ofthose.com

Alec Motyer

44 UNDATED DEVOTIONS THROUGH THE BOOK OF DEUTERONOMY

INTRODUCTION

The opening verses of Deuteronomy tell us all we need to know about the book we are about to read. Moses and Israel are in the land of Moab, poised to cross the Jordan and take possession of the land the Lord promised as an inheritance. Moses has some final words to say to them, which Deuteronomy faithfully records for our learning.

Deuteronomy comes to us in carefully edited form. Note the editorial introductions: 'These are the words' (1:1); 'This is the law' (4:44); 'These are the terms' (literally, 'words', 29:1); 'This is the blessing' (33:1); also see 31:1 and 31:30. The opening chapters (1:1 - 4:43) are an historical retrospect of the journey from Sinai to the second arrival at the borders of Canaan. The great central section (4:44 - 26:19) is a meditative application of the Decalogue, sometimes taking up one or other of the commandments with great force and clarity, often circling round the area of conduct to which a commandment is relevant, but all the time enforcing the fundamental obligations of Israel within the covenant. The separate introduction in 27:1 marks out chapters 27–31 as underlining, in particular, the blessings and curses of the covenant - a powerful summons to choose life, and a provision for regular public reading of the covenant law. Finally, chapters 32–34 are a retrospective of Moses, with his final words and wishes, then the death of the great leader. Much closer analysis of content is possible (and convincing) but would only be confusing in the brief compass of an introduction like this. Hopefully enough has been offered here to keep you broadly aware of your place in this great book of the Bible.

Much ink has been spilt linking Deuteronomy with 'the book of the Law' found in the house of the Lord in the days of Josiah (2 Kings 22), and many have even urged that Deuteronomy owed its origin to that event, being produced in order to promote Josiah's reformation. All this remains highly suppositional - indeed it would not be hard to show how, for example, Leviticus would be equally appropriate to Josiah. Deuteronomy is best understood by the setting it proposes for itself: the final addresses of Moses to the people he has loved, cherished and lead for the last forty years.

The book and its message

These verses are a preface to the whole book and, in principle, tell us all we need to know. Three times Moses is named as its author (vv. 1, 3, 5). It was Moses who 'spoke to all Israel' (v. 1); what Moses said the Lord had already said to him (v. 3): the voice was human, the words divine. Moses was a prophet (cf. 34:10), and, like all the prophets, he could say, 'Thus says the Lord', meaning, 'If the Lord had chosen to come in person to speak to you instead of sending me, this is, word for word, what he would have said.' This is the miracle of Bible inspiration: human speech and divine word. Moses' task was also to 'make plain' God's law (v. 5; for the verb see 27:8; Hab. 2:2).

Notice how the preface insists on telling us where Moses spoke (v. 1), when he spoke (vv. 2–3a), as well as how he spoke (with clarification, v. 5). The rest of Deuteronomy will demonstrate the accuracy of that verb 'make clear'. The man who started out 'slow of speech and tongue' (Ex. 4:10) found God to be as good as his word to be 'with' Moses' mouth (Ex. 4:12), and he became the scintillating orator we find in this book. But the 'where' and 'when' are important too. They were in the wilderness. Deuteronomy is a book for the Lord's people still in this world, surrounded by named locations with all their peoples, potential opposition, possible temptations and trials.

This, indeed, is the point of the exact dating (Deut. 1:2–3a) of Moses' words. A journey that could have been accomplished in eleven days (v. 2) took nigh on forty years (v. 3a)! Moses will himself tell us more about this at the end of chapter 1: they had come, forty years earlier, to the border of Canaan and refused to obey the voice of the Lord. Disobedience costs! That is part of the message of Deuteronomy – to us as to our ancestors of old.

But there is a date attached also to 'how' Moses spoke (v. 4) – it was after the defeat of Sihon and Og. They were the awesome kings ruling in Transjordan (Num. 21:21–35) who fell before an Israel that believed the Lord's promise 'I have delivered him into your hand'. In other words, disobedience costs but obedience rewards. Deuteronomy develops these truths in many ways, but, at heart, the position is that the Lord's people possess the Lord's commands (Deut. 1:3), their hallmark is to obey them, and this is the way of blessing.

REFLECTION

Remember what benefits the Lord's word bestows (Ps. 19:7–11).

DAY 2

READ Deuteronomy 1:6–21

The word of God for the whole of life

Moses is looking back over the last forty years (v. 3) and recalling (vv. 6–8) the exciting, key moment when they left Sinai for the desert journey to Canaan. How memories must have flooded back! But one event stands out in his mind: how he picked out leaders of thousands, hundreds, fifties and tens (v. 15). What a let-down! What a dull thing to remember out of all that thrilling time! (See Ex. 18 for how it happened.) But historians only pick out what they think is important. That's their job – to focus on the really significant among the loads of facts and figures available to them. So we must ask what was special about this series of appointments.

Look first at the way this whole section is planned. It begins and ends (vv. 6–8, 21) with the command to 'go ... and take possession'. This is the 'bracket' or 'inclusion' around the verses. Within the brackets we find the record of appointing the leaders. In other words, the leaders and their work is the link between the setting out and actually entering to possess. In Exodus 18:15, Moses said the people came to him 'to seek God's will', and it was this function he passed on to the chosen leaders when he counselled them that 'judgment belongs to God' (Deut. 1:17).

To 'judge' in the Old Testament means to give an authoritative decision settling some issue. It was the judges' task to keep the people on track with the word of God, and this was the point of having leaders available to local or family groups (tens), area groups (fifties and hundreds) and major tribal divisions (thousands). The word of God had to be readily available in every situation, however widespread and however localised. This was the way Moses did it, and he was insistent about it. According to verse 16, their 'judgment' was for all without exception – whether a brother or a stranger. It was to be without fear or favour (v. 17), with no partiality. And it was to be without deviation from 'everything' they'd been told (v. 18). When he appointed the leaders, Moses did relieve himself of intense pressures but that was not the point. The point was doing everything possible to make and keep them as the people of the word of the Lord.

REFLECTION

Between setting out and arriving, all we need is the word of God.

Getting stuck

According to verse 19, the Israelites started out for the Promised Land from Kadesh Barnea; verse 46 tells us that was where they ended. It's the story of a people who got stuck! What was meant to be a springboard to blessing (v. 22) became the location and punishment of failure (v. 46).

Now how did that happen? Well, look at an interesting contrast. In verses 6–21 the people begin (vv. 6–8) and end (vv. 19–21) following God, and in between (vv. 9–18) they obey God under the guidance of their appointed 'judges'. But in verses 22–46 they begin (vv. 22–25) and end (vv. 41–46) following man, and in between (vv. 26–40) they rebel (v. 26), grumble (v. 27), do not trust (v. 32) and, consequently, are sent back into the wilderness (v. 40).

It is so often like this in the Bible: when we see the pattern, we see the message. A people under the word of God are in the way of blessing; a people turning from the word of God are the architects of their own loss and deprivation. By refusing to enter the land (vv. 25–26) the Israelites were in effect choosing the wilderness – and they got what they chose.

The heart of the matter was disobedience to God's word – this is why the significant reference to Moses, Caleb and Joshua lies at the centre of today's reading (vv. 36–38). They are a case in point. Moses had committed his own disobedience (Num. 20:7–12) and paid the penalty, on 'your account' (Deut. 3:26, NKJV) – so that people would see what a serious offence it is to disobey; Caleb and Joshua had stood up against the rebels (Num. 14:6–9) and were rewarded for their obedience (Deut. 1:35–36, 38).

Disobedience has various facets. It began with the Israelites' logical plan to send spies (v. 22). They requested 'men' to go ahead of them – as if the Lord had not led them safely thus far! Was the pillar of cloud and fire not enough (Ex. 40:38)? Human reliance replaced spiritual trust. Reliance on human wisdom soon became stubborn resistance (Deut. 1:26), digging in one's heels against God's command, discontent (v. 27) and – the sin of sins – abandonment of the way of faith (v. 32).

REFLECTION

The Lord is unchanging in power (v. 30), in love (v. 31) and in care (vv. 32–33).

Lessons to be learned

In the course of the forty years that began at 2:1, crowds of people were caught up in the consequences of the sin of disobedience for which they could not be blamed – they had to wait for every one of that 'evil generation' to die (1:35) before they could enter the land (1:39). They would have been very different from us if they had never thought, 'What have we done to deserve this – the inhospitable desert year after year!' People often say that the Bible does not explain suffering, but that is not so; it offers many explanations – only they are not the sort of 'explanation' we think we need! Would Israel have learned in any other way the lesson of steady obedience?

The command (2:4) was obeyed (v. 8); command and obedience went together (v. 13). When the Lord said, 'Do not provoke' (v. 5; cf. v. 9), they did not provoke. When he said, 'cross' (v. 13), they crossed over. Was there any other way they could have learned so vividly and effectively the loving, daily care of their God (v. 7; cf. 8:2–4)? They learned to live within the sovereign plan of God – indeed, if they did not know it already, they learned that he is sovereign over all the nations of the world.

Notice the repeated 'not give ... have given ...' (vv. 5, 9, 19) and finally, the decisive 'have given' in relation to the dreaded king Sihon (v. 24). The Lord is a sovereign God indeed who does what he pleases in heaven and earth (Ps. 135:6). They learned that he is to be trusted when he says, 'Do not' (Deut. 1:5, 9); he is to be trusted for daily needs (v. 7); and he is to be trusted for the future – the Anakim were a danger lying ahead (1:28) which would have to be faced, but history showed that even such people were vulnerable under the hand of the Lord (2:10–12, 20).

Hebrews 5:8 says of the Lord Jesus that he 'learned obedience from what he suffered'. So did Israel in the forty years of wilderness discipline – lessons which, very likely, could not have been so well learned in any other way. In the hand of God everything has its time and purpose.

REFLECTION

Think about 2 Corinthians 4:17–18. The NKJV has the correct translation of verse 18: 'while we do not look at ... but at ...'

DAY 5

READ Deuteronomy 2:26 – 3:11

'The clouds you so much dread'

Seven times the Hebrew verb 'to give' occurs in this passage (see the ESV; the NKJV translates it as 'deliver' four times). The land is a gift (2:29), so are Sihon (2:31) and Og (3:2–3) and the surrounding Transjordanian lands (2:36). Wherever the people looked they saw what the Lord had given. As they looked forward, the human eye saw two extremely powerful monarchs – Sihon and Og – but the instructed eye saw what was about to be 'given'. As they looked back, they saw that it was indeed so: the dreaded kings (cf. 3:11) were gone – given and delivered over by divine gift and power. And over the Jordan awaited the richest gift of all: the Promised Land (2:29).

Now look at other verbs in the passage: 'we struck him down' (2:33); we 'took' or 'carried off' (2:34, 35; 3:4, 7, 8); 'we struck' (3:3); and 'we completely destroyed' (3:6). Interestingly, then, we have seven references to 'gift' and eight references to fighting, conquering and so on. If the land became theirs by military effort and prowess, how was it a gift? If it was a gift, why did they need to fight? We face here the difference between conversion and sanctification. Exodus 14:13 says, 'Stand still, and see the salvation of the LORD' (ESV; cf. 14:14). Salvation is all of God in the absolute sense of Titus 3:5: 'He saved us'. Holiness is also God's absolute gift in Christ (1 Cor. 1:30), but we enter into it on different terms. As God's regenerate ones – born again and alive from the dead (Eph. 2:1, 5) – he looks to us to show signs of life (just as we might ask, 'Is the baby walking yet?')

So, for our ancestors of old, they entered into the enjoyment of the gift by their commitment to the battle. They were not earning their salvation; they were enjoying their status, privileges and blessings as the saved. It is in this spirit that David can say the Lord trains his hands for war and his fingers to fight (Ps. 144:1). In the same way, Acts 5:32 speaks of 'the Holy Spirit, whom God has given to those who obey him'. Obedience, in the regenerate, is a means of grace. Jesus himself says, 'If you love me, you will obey what I command' (John 14:15) – obedience is a proof of love – and 'I will ask the Father, and he will give you another Counsellor' (John 14:16) – obedience is a means of grace.

REFLECTION

Consider that born-again Christians are likened to soldiers, athletes and farmers (2 Tim. 2:3–6).

DAY 6

READ Deuteronomy 3:12–29

Giving and withholding

Moses was understandably sensitive when faced with the possibility of two and a half tribes peeling off from the total company to settle outside the Promised Land (see Num. 32:6–15). He laid down two safeguarding conditions: no fracturing of the unity of the people, and nothing less than total mobilisation for the war of possession (v. 18).

Both of these truths are important, and their lessons carry over into the New Testament. We have inevitably become accustomed to the denominational divisions we have inherited – and can even rejoice in them as if disunity did not matter – but John 17:21 urges unity. Even more sadly we acquiesce in divisions within the local fellowship – and proceed to take sides. (Someone in our village shop chortled publicly, 'I hear they are at each other's throats again down at the church!') But Moses insisted that nothing less than the total, united mobilisation of the people of the Lord will bring about possession of their God-intended possessions. The battle to enter into what God has given – the battle for sanctification – demands everything we can give (Heb. 12:4).

The highly personal verses 21–27 are equally important. Moses failed to be sensitive to the minutiae of obedience (cf. Num. 20:8, 11). He did not lose his salvation (cf. 1 Cor. 3:15; Luke 9:30–31), but he did lose the joy and privilege of leading the people into their inheritance. He felt the divine anger 'on your account' (Deut. 3:26, NKJV) – because of what the Lord purposed for you: that you should know the fearful consequences of disobedience, and also how detailed our obedience should be. But, in all this, the Lord still pursues his purposes undaunted, and the word is to 'encourage and strengthen' Joshua for the unchanged task ahead (v. 28). 'I the LORD do not change. So you, O descendants of Jacob, are not destroyed' (Mal. 3:6). And Joshua's 'encouragement' is ours too: what the Lord has been in the past is a revelation of what he is, and an assurance of what he will do in the future (Deut. 3:21). The God of our salvation is the God we need for tomorrow.

REFLECTION

Unity (Phil. 1:27; 4:2), mobilisation (Eph. 6:13) and wholeheartedness (Col. 3:23) are the continuing 'marks' of the Lord's people.

The magnetic people

Deuteronomy 4 is a central statement of the message of Deuteronomy, and deserves close thought. Today's verses are in four sections: verses 1–5 offer a basic principle; verses 5, 9 and 15 introduce three 'cautions' to safeguard this principle.

The people of God have and hold the word of God. This is their distinguishing mark – where the word of God is, there the people of God are – and honouring and guarding this word is their first duty. It is a word with a human voice and a divine origin (vv. 1, 5). Verse 1 shows us further that obedience to the word is the key to life ('live'), progress ('go in'), and possession/victory ('take possession'). It is designed for obedience, and is to be guarded against addition or subtraction (v. 2). Its dominance in the life of the people is always tested (vv. 3–4; cf. Mark 4:17). The Lord's people are not seekers after the truth – they already possess it – but are researchers and guardians of given truth. What Moses thus said and claimed for the words he mediated, we assert of the whole Bible.

Now for the first of the three 'cautions': Israel is a magnetic people (vv. 6–8). When the Lord's people are known for their devotion to his word (vv. 6, 8), and when the Lord's presence among them is displayed by their commitment to solving their problems by prayer and by his answers (v. 7), they become a magnet to the watching world. 'Near' (v. 7) is part of the 'next-of-kin' vocabulary of the Old Testament: the Lord has, in grace, related himself in the closest terms to us.

Secondly, the unique word (vv. 9–14). Looking back to the basic Sinai revelation of God (Ex. 19), yes, there was fire, cloud and darkness, but it was by God's word alone that the Lord made himself and his will known. His word was spoken in perpetuity (v.9). The actual words were from God himself (vv. 10, 12), given for their obedience (v. 13) and mediated intact through Moses (v. 14).

Thirdly, the irreplaceable word (vv. 15–20). There was a total embargo on any and every sort of visual representation of the Lord. All such represent merely human ideas (v. 16), or draw on created life – and therefore what is beneath God in glory (vv. 17–18). Even the most exalted aspects of the creation would only serve to reduce the Lord's people to the level of the nations from whom he has separated them to belong to him alone (vv. 19, 20).

REFLECTION

Only Jesus is the image of the invisible God (John 12:42–50; 14:9; Col. 1:15–18).

On being unique

In the beautiful way Moses' sermon in Deuteronomy 4 is presented, verses 32–38 take up the theme of Israel being a unique people, matching the same theme in verses 5–20; the call to obedience in verses 39–40 matches the call in verses 1–5; and verses 21–31 at the centre emphasise they mustn't disobey. Please read the whole sermon with this outline in mind. It is a great piece of literature and a real treat.

There are some strands of truth that come in for special emphasis. First, and foremost, there is the fact of special revelation: God revealed his truth in his own words (vv. 1–2, 5, 10, 12–15, 36, 40). He spoke through Moses, but the words that came naturally to Moses were the very words the Lord would have used had he spoken in his own person. This is the miracle of 'verbal inspiration'.

Secondly, the Lord, Yahweh, is revealed as the only God (vv. 35, 39) – a God of fiery holiness (vv. 11–12, 36), burning with the fire of true love and expressing himself in jealousy to have the full affection of his people (v. 24), so consequently a God of wrath against sin (v. 3, 26). Yet, at the same time, he is a God responding in mercy (v. 31) to repentance (vv. 29–30). Why then, we might ask, was not Moses forgiven and restored at once (vv. 21–22)? His own answer is that the Lord acted 'on your account' (3:26, NKJV), meaning 'out of consideration for you'. The people had to be taught the seriousness of disobedience, and the Lord chose to do this through the example of Moses – not by injustice, however, because Moses, we may say, only received the due reward of his deeds.

Thirdly, matching the only God, there is the unique people (vv. 7–8, 20, 33–34, 37–38) – unique in their possession of a revealed way of life and a power of prayer. They are separated from the nations (v. 20) by their possession of revealed truth (v. 33) and their unique way of salvation (v. 34), and their deliverance was by his personal presence (v. 37; literally, 'his face' – all he had to do was show his face!) and mighty victories (v. 38).

Fourthly, this relationship was sealed by a covenant (vv. 23, 31), which involved, among all else in the way of life it commanded, a strict rule of 'imageless' worship (vv. 15–18, 23). Fifthly, and finally, children were underlined as especially important within the covenant family (vv. 9, 25, 40; cf. Ex. 12:26–27), with a parental obligation to teach the coming generations.

REFLECTION

Dwell on the fact the Bible is God's revealed word (2 Tim. 3:16–17; 2 Pet.1:19–21).

DAY 9

READ Deuteronomy 4:44 – 5:33

What the Lord actually said

Moses describes the Lord's word to Israel, in 4:44–45, as 'law', i.e., *teaching*; as 'stipulations' (or 'testimony'), i.e., what God *witnesses to* as the truth about himself and his desires; as 'decrees' (or 'statutes'), a word related to the verb 'to engrave', therefore pointing to *permanency*; and as 'laws' (or 'judgments'), that is, what God has *authoritatively decided upon* as the truth to hold and the life to live. In 4:40 Moses adds 'commands' – God's word is designed *for our obedience*.

The required response is given in 5:1: to 'hear' (i.e., to open the ears, mind and heart); to 'learn' (i.e., to take on board, store away and make part of the fabric of one's thinking); and to 'follow' (literally, 'to keep by doing') – not simply with the duty of a trustee but with the obedience of a servant. In 5:33 Moses adds the command to 'walk' – we are to make God's word our habitual practice, with its attached promise of life (a 'life ... to the full', John 10:10) and security of tenure of the gifts of God.

All these descriptions, commands and promises are linked with the Ten Commandments (5:6–21), which verse 22 then identifies as what God actually said, laid down in writing as a permanent deposit of truth and obligation for his people. Here is one way of seeing the Decalogue as a complete rounded statement:

1. Spiritual (commandments 1–4)
   a. Thoughts (1–2); b. words (3);
   c. deeds (4)
2. Domestic (commandment 5)
3. Social (commandments 6–10)
   a. Deeds (6–8); b. words (9);
   c. thoughts (10).

It is not true to say the commandments only deal with externalities, awaiting Jesus to extend them to our thoughts (Matt. 5:22, 28). They begin and end inwardly with how we think about the Lord. Has he our sole loyalty (commandment 1)? What thoughts dominate our minds in worship (2)? How are we thinking about our neighbours and their possessions (10)? The emphasis laid on our domestic life (5) matches the different way this command is expressed. After our obligations to God (1–4), our primary duty begins at home (5).

The main difference between the commandments given in Deuteronomy and in Exodus 20, touches on the fourth commandment where we are called, in Exodus, to follow the Creator's pattern of work, and, in Deuteronomy, to respond to the Redeemer's work of deliverance.

REFLECTION

Delight in God's teaching: 'Oh, how I love your law!' (Ps. 119:97).

READ Deuteronomy 6:1–9

One Lord, one pre-occupation

Right at the heart of today's verses is what became the great credal statement: 'Yahweh our God, Yahweh is one.' The word translated 'one' is worth considering. There is a Hebrew word, *yachiydh*, to depict what is unique – the one and only one or a bare unit that admits no addition or multiplication. It is used, for example, of Isaac in Genesis 22:2. But in Deuteronomy 6:4, Yahweh is called *echadh*, which allows for a wider range of significance. In Exodus 26:6, for example, the tabernacle is described as 'one', that is to say it is a multiple unity – a bringing together of a huge number of individual, different parts into a glorious 'oneness'.

The Old Testament introduces us to a number of divine personages: the Angel of Yahweh, the Word of Yahweh, the Spirit of Yahweh. Indeed one of its favourite titles is 'Yahweh of Hosts', implying that within his oneness Yahweh holds together a host of potentialities and powers – we are to understand his oneness as multiple: his is a complex and wonderful unity. This is part of the Old Testament preparation for the New Testament revelation of God as the Holy Trinity where Yahweh's unity is that of the Father, the Son and the Holy Spirit. But, of course, Yahweh is one too in the sense that there is no other God.

Consequently our verses insist on a parallel exclusive commitment to him: he is the only One; he calls for our total and exclusive devotion. He has spoken (v. 1); we obey (v. 2). He is the only One (v. 4); he calls for our whole heart and soul (vv. 5–6) – the total commitment of our mental and emotional natures, devoted to him with all our 'strength' (that is, our energy, enthusiasm and gusto). He is One, therefore he looks for our domestic commitment – in what we teach our children (v. 7a) and the chosen topic of conversation in the home (v. 7b), from morning to night (v. 7c). His word is to guide what we do (our 'hands', v. 8), what we aim at in life (between our 'eyes', v. 8, NKJV) as well as the direction in which our eyes direct our feet. He is to be our public testimony (v. 9). The co-relative of One God is a one-track mind!

REFLECTION

What makes heaven perfect in every way is its exclusive focus on the throne of God and of the Lamb (Rev. 5:8–13).

DAY 11

READ Deuteronomy 6:10–25

The inheritors

At its start (v. 10), its ending (v. 23) and its centre (v. 18) this section announces one theme: people are being 'brought into' the Promised Land (v. 10), to possess it (v. 18), having been brought out in order to be brought in (v. 23). It is all the Lord's purpose for his people – not at all of their doing (v. 11) but the gift of God (v. 23). Yet what sort of people Israel are is far from treated as unimportant. They inherit by gift, but are called to display the characteristics which show that they are indeed inheritors. There are seven characteristics mentioned:

1. The Lord's salvation always kept in their minds – they were saved from Egypt and bondage (v. 12).
2. Awareness of God's greatness and holiness, reflected in 'fear' or reverential awe (v. 13).
3. Devotion to the Lord's service and worship (v. 13). Here 'serve' includes whatever service he commands and also, like our word today, 'holding a service' or religious worship.
4. Pledging loyalty to him (v. 13). Here 'take ... oaths' is in the sense of making a commitment to him and affirming devotion.
5. Exclusive commitment and thus distinctive separation from other loyalties (v. 14). This means division from other gods, other people and the 'religious' demands of alternative objects of worship, as well as from the distinctive practices of their devotees.
6. Simple, unquestioning trust in the Lord's promises (v. 16). Here to 'test' God involves withholding trust in any given situation until he 'proves himself' trustworthy. In contrast, proper trust always says, 'His love in time past forbids me to think he'll leave me at last in trouble to sink.'
7. Possessing and obeying God's word (vv. 17–18).

Are all these of equal importance? Fundamentally, yes, nevertheless two are underlined by having supplements attached to them. The 'sole loyalty' theme of verse 14 is amplified by the insistence in verse 15 that the Lord's love is a true love, therefore comes with its essential component of jealous longing to have the full response of the loved one. The call for obedience to God's word (vv. 17–18) is reiterated in verses 24–25. Living by the word of God is living in God-pleasing righteousness – not trying to earn righteousness by the way we live but displaying righteousness because we are already 'right with him'.

REFLECTION

'Peacemakers who sow in peace raise a harvest of righteousness' (Jas. 3:18).

READ Deuteronomy 7:1–11

Into battle, part 1: *know your enemy, know your God*

There are many repetitions in Deuteronomy. We must never say, 'We've read all this before', but rather, 'It must be important to merit repeating.' 6:10 says, 'the LORD your God brings you into ... to give you ...'; 7:1–2 says, 'the LORD your God brings you into ... and when ... you have defeated them ...' The difference is not of fact but of emphasis. Being brought out of Egypt represents the work of salvation, therefore, 'Stand firm and you will see' (Ex. 14:13). Yet once we are saved we are alive from the dead (Eph. 2:4–6), and we are called to show signs of life ('to live', Eph. 4:1; literally, to 'walk'), to put on armour (Eph. 6:11), to run so as to win (1 Cor. 9:24) and to resist even to the point of shedding blood (Heb. 12:4).

The objective (our 'war aim') is to establish and maintain our status as a distinct people (Deut. 7:2–5). Of course we are not called to 'destroy ... totally' (v. 2) – that was right for its own time – but we are called to display a similar zeal to maintain our separateness and distinctiveness, avoiding entangling relationships (v. 2), including marriage (v. 3), and shunning everything that imperils our sole loyalty to the Lord (v. 6).

Why are we to be intent on these positive differences? Because the Lord has dealt differently with us (vv. 6–10). 'Holy' (v. 6) means 'separate', in the sense of positively belonging to a different sphere of reality, God's reality; it's being different because we belong to him. This is why the sex worker of Genesis 38 can be called 'the holy woman' (v. 21, literally) – because she belonged to Baal, lived in his sphere of reality, and served him as he required. We are separated for God because of his choice (Deut. 7:7; Eph. 1:4), which arose from his unexplained love (Deut. 7:8; Eph. 2:4), itself an expression of his faithfulness to his promises and displayed in his work of salvation (Deut. 7:8).

Deuteronomy sums all this up as God's faithfulness, his loyalty to promises made (the covenant) and his undying, unchanging, steadfast, covenant love. 'Set his affection' (v. 7) is a phrase that could be used of 'falling in love' (cf. Gen. 34:8) while 'love' (v. 9) is the love that pledges unchanging devotion 'till death us do part' – the contrast is between love as an expression of the emotions and love as a commitment of the will.

REFLECTION

To say, 'He loves because he loves' (vv. 7–8) is as far as we are allowed to press into the divine will. It implies there are very good reasons for all he does – but he is not telling us!

DAY 13

READ Deuteronomy 7:12–26

Into battle, part 2: *not fearing, but listening, remembering, expecting*

The Bible is so focused on its history writing that we can easily forget that, as regards Deuteronomy for example, the whole land of Canaan was thickly populated, highly organised, well led, and, according to the standards of the time, armed to the teeth. It was no small act of faith to believe the Lord had given it over to Israel to possess, and no small undertaking to march in to conquer and possess it. Moses did well to recognise that his people needed to be guarded against the paralysis of fear (vv. 17–18).

First, we see the word of God is the guarantee of present divine care (vv. 12–15) and victory (v. 16). The verbs in verse 12 ('pay attention ... are careful to follow') offer a programme of patient hearing, committed guarding and practical obeying – literally, 'listen ... keep ... do'. For the Canaanites, enjoying the blessing of the 'gods' arose from 'working the system'. 'Baal' was the in effect the description of impersonal processes of fertility/prosperity – like 'market forces' today – and there were mechanisms for getting Baal 'on side' and reaping the benefit in good crops, fine animals and many children. The benefits of divine care in Israel, however, were consequent on moral submission to the word of God (vv. 12–16).

Secondly, the acts of God in the past are the guarantee of present interventions (vv. 17–19). Whatever situation we face, we should start the counteroffensive by giving ourselves the tonic of remembering what the Lord has done: both what he did to his opponents (v. 18 – and Pharaoh was the superpower of the day!) and what he did for us when he brought us out of bondage into salvation (v.19 – and we were totally helpless!). In that same verse, the 'trials' or testings were the successive plagues by which God showed his command of the 'forces' of creation; 'signs' are acts that point away from themselves to the truth they demonstrate; and 'wonders' are acts that call attention, making people stop and question. Memory stimulates faith.

Thirdly, notice the three 'your God will' statements (vv. 20, 22, 23). 'Hornet' (v. 20) is a dubious translation but, whatever the meaning, the sense remains: the Lord goes before, preparing our way into his promises. It is he who overcomes (v. 22) and brings us into possession (v. 23).We gratefully remember what he has done in the past; his power will bring us to possess our possessions in the future.

REFLECTION

God does not change therefore we are not consumed (Mal. 3:6).

Through all the changing scenes of life

Life changes; the Lord does not change. Why was Israel in the wilderness? The Lord led them there (v. 2). Why would they enjoy prosperity in Canaan? The Lord brought them in (v. 7). He is never anywhere else than caring for his people. No other mind plans for them; no other hand cares for them. This is one of the great themes in Deuteronomy 8.

Parallel to it is the second theme: our minds must be equally concentrated on him. We are urged to be careful 'to remember' (v. 2) and 'Be careful that you do not forget' (v. 11). *Trials bring blessings* (vv. 2–6): a right lowly understanding of ourselves (v. 2a), a heart tested for loyalty (v. 2b), sufficient provision in every situation (vv. 3–4) and divine education (v. 5). *Prosperity brings snares* (vv. 7–17): forgetting God and slackness in obeying (v. 11), arrogance and a wrong understanding of ourselves (vv. 14, 17).

When life is difficult, people say, 'But I do not see the point!' Yet equally we should wonder what the point is of the good times – though, in our unthinking way, we don't! But our God of grace is always purposeful in all his dealings: he is working to draw out our hearts in devotion to himself (v. 2), to teach us proper priorities for life and to rebuke our materialism (v. 3), to educate us as a father trains his sons (v. 5; cf. Heb. 12:5–11) and to bring us to the good he intends for us but which can be reached by no other way (v. 15 – there was no other way from Egypt to Canaan but through the wilderness). It's like the parable of the weeds (Matt. 13:24–30, 36–43): weed them out early and the wheat will be damaged in the process and not become perfect to harvest.

There is a third great theme running through Deuteronomy 8. Verses 2, 5, 14 and 17 (where 'to yourself' literally means 'in your heart') all mention the heart as a key personal factor – the heart set to obey (v. 2), the heart that goes on trusting the Father's wisdom 'in all the changing scenes of life' (v. 5), the heart guarded against forgetting (v. 14), and the heart exercised in remembrance and thankfulness (v. 18). Such a heart sings with the hymn-writer, 'What didst thou find in me that thou hast dealt so lovingly'[1] and knows the answer – nothing! It is all of God, all of grace, all of goodness and all of his determination to honour his own covenant (v. 18).

REFLECTION

Rejoice that: 'Through all the changing scenes of life, in trouble or in joy, the praises of my God shall still my heart and tongue employ'[2] (based on Ps. 34:1–8).

DAY 15

READ Deuteronomy 9:1–29

The inflexible God of salvation

We should really read chapters 9 and 10 together so as to see clearly that not even the great sin of the golden calf (9:12, 16, 21) deflects the Lord from his redemptive purpose. Rather he commanded new tablets (10:1) and repeated his written law (10:4), he listened to prayer for mercy (10:10), and commanded the forward journey to the Promised Land (10:11).

This same great truth is implicit though in chapter 9 when taken alone. It opens with the great assurance of coming inheritance (v. 1), notwithstanding the potential difficulties (v. 2), and then commands understanding of the Lord's purpose (vv. 3–6), warns against forgetfulness of how things really are (vv. 7–24) and finally recalls the outcome they deserve (vv. 25–29). The whole chapter is, in fact, an assertion that salvation has to be all of God – or, putting the truth in biblical perspective, that salvation is all of grace from beginning to end.

First, *salvation is not because of your righteousness* (vv. 1–6). What is really worked out here is that the Lord's work of salvation for his people is consistent with his moral rule over the whole world. At the start, bringing his people out of Egypt involved the overthrow Egypt deserved – as Exodus shows; bringing them into Canaan involved dispossessing the Canaanites – which is what, by then, they deserved (Gen. 15:16).

Second, *salvation is in spite of your sinfulness and unworthiness* (Deut. 9:7–23). In these verses there are at least fifteen recollections of provocation, rebellion, turning aside, acting corruptly, sin and disobedience. It all came to a head in the sin of the golden calf, but it had characterised them from the start (v. 7) – and was present even at the climax of their privileged receiving of God's law at Horeb, otherwise known as Sinai (v. 8) – and at each stage of the journey (v. 22) – again climaxing at Kadesh Barnea when they refused to invade Canaan (v. 23).

Thirdly, *salvation is contrary to what you deserve* (vv. 24–39). Rightly, the Lord threatened destruction, a fate from which Israel was saved when Moses pleaded on the basis of what the Lord had already done (v. 26), what he had promised the forefathers (v. 27) and what his own good name merited (v. 28).

REFLECTION

Ezekiel 20:1–44 reviews the history of Israel. Its storyline is 'I acted for my name's sake' (vv. 9, 14, 22, 44).

Two unchangeable things

We have already noticed how surprising chapter 10 is. After all that chapter 9 has recorded – Israel's unrighteousness, sinfulness and unworthiness – things continue as before! The Lord does not change course or make adjustments in his purposes. We should learn to marvel at this – with wonder, love and praise. It is what we mean by 'the faithfulness of God'. Two things in particular we should note. First, his law does not change – with his own hand he writes exactly what he had written the first time (vv. 1–11, particularly vv. 2, 4). Secondly, the call to live according to his law does not change (vv. 12–22).

In each of these sections there is a potent and important symbol. In the first, Moses makes a direct link between the giving of the law and the making of the ark (vv. 2–3, 4–5). The law is not received till its 'home' is ready; it is not simply deposited with Israel but housed in the special box. Exodus 25:16–21 directs that the tablets of the law are perpetually under the atonement cover (or mercy seat, NKJV); Leviticus 16:14–17 directs that the blood of atonement be sprinkled on the atonement cover. The Lord's people are always under his law; and his law is always under the atoning blood. The call to obey and the provision for disobedience cannot ever be separated (cf. 1 John 1:7).

The powerful symbol in the second half of the chapter is circumcision (v. 16). According to Genesis 17 there are two aspects to the Lord's covenant. It is, first, a series of promises (domestic, v. 2; national, v. 4; personal, v. 5; royal, v. 6; spiritual, v. 7; territorial, v. 8). Secondly, it is ceremonial (vv. 9–14). Circumcision marks out the people to whom these great promises have been made, or, to put it differently, it marks out those who are within the covenant, with all its promises of transforming grace and blessing. The call in Deuteronomy is, 'Circumcise your hearts' (10:16): we are to bring all our capacities of thought, emotion, mind, will and imagination – all that is within us (cf. Prov. 4:23) – within the embrace of God's all-sufficient grace, so as to obey his law, love his name, reverence him and give him our total loyalty.

REFLECTION

All of God's children have hearts that have been circumcised by the Spirit of Christ (Romans 2:28–29; Col. 2:11).

The conclusion of the matter

Chapter 11 is the climax and conclusion of the first section of Deuteronomy. It summarises the main point of Moses' teaching so far, and does so in three sections: the past (vv. 1–9) – all they have seen the Lord do for them; the future (vv. 10–25), as they go forward into Canaan – and find themselves in a new and different situation; and the unchanging, ongoing present (vv. 26–32) – something that is to be their ever-present, fixed reality in their new life. The common thread binding these sections together is the word of God – God's own word (v. 1), commanded by and through Moses (vv. 8, 18, 22). It is the key to personal maturity, progress and tenure (vv. 8–9); the basis of a loving relationship with the Lord (v. 13); the dominant factor in personal and family life (vv. 18–19); and the way of victory and advancement (vv. 22–25).

Life in Egypt was dominated by the ever-flowing Nile, whose waters were carried throughout fertile Egypt in manmade leats and channels, some of the latter being so small that they could be either blocked or opened by heaping or removing soil by foot (v. 10). It would not be so in Canaan. Life would depend on rainfall (v. 11), a gift God grants to obedient people (vv. 13–14).

Similarly, Canaanites practised what is called 'imitative magic' – doing on earth what one desired the 'god' to do from heaven. For this reason the 'worship' of Baal included human sexual acts of fertility. It would not be so for Israel. Life and fertility had a moral and spiritual basis in possessing and obeying the word of God. Furthermore, when Israel entered Canaan, among their first acts was to seek out two mountains in the centre of the land (v. 29) and identify them with life (Gerizim) and death (Ebal), the respective consequences of obeying or disobeying the Lord's word (vv. 27–28). The very fabric of their new land was to be identified with the call to obey and the warning against disobeying. It was the setting and framework, the context in which they lived and the unchanging constitution of being Israel, the possessor of divine revelation.

REFLECTION

As Christians, 'continue in what you have learned ... All scripture ...' (2 Tim. 3:14–16). Our Bibles are our Mounts Gerizim and Ebal.

DAY 18

READ Deuteronomy 12:1–32

No other name

According to the introduction in 1:5, Moses was teaching (as the word 'law' means). In particular he was teaching the great, fundamental principle of Israel's life: obedience to the word of God. From 12:1 onwards (to 26:19) he is dealing with 'decrees and laws' – the commands of God in their unchangeable nature ('decrees' are, literally, statutes, engraved in the rock for permanence) and their divine origin ('laws' here are, literally, judgments: the authoritative decisions and pronouncements of the divine Judge-King). These rules are to be practised in everyday life.

Chapter 12 can be seen as an application of the first two commandments: there is only one God and one exclusive object of worship. It will help our reading if we see how carefully planned this chapter is. Verses 1–4 affirm the principle of *exclusivity*, and this is repeated in the matching verses 29–32 (compare verses 4 and 31). In verses 5–14 (note how these two end verses have the same theme, bracketing the section), the truth of one only God is reflected in the provision of one central place and focus of worship. Verses 15–19 and 20–28 cover the same ground twice: first, domestic meat-eating is allowed, provided the sacredness of the blood is guarded (vv. 15–16 and vv. 20–25); secondly, the statutory offerings must be brought to the chosen place (vv. 17–19 and vv. 26–28).

In a day like ours, when 'inclusivity' is all the rage – with interfaith services where each 'faith community' contributes its own 'insights' – it would be easy to take offence at the rigid exclusivity of Deuteronomy (vv. 2–3, 30–31). No, of course we are not called to go around demolishing things, but the inescapable fact is that the Bible does not see all other religions as 'equal', with each having a bit of truth and none having it all. There is religious falsehood in the world and, Bible in hand, we are called to keep clear and pure from it. The great truth of only one God should be unmistakable in our worship. Likewise, our worship should be a time of rejoicing (vv. 7, 12, 18). Even the idea of a single 'chosen place' speaks to us. Not now an earthly site, involving great journeys, our 'chosen place' – the centre our God has appointed for us, where his Name dwells – is Jesus (John 2:21).

REFLECTION

Ask these questions of your worship: does it truly reflect your belief that there is only one God and no other? Does it – please be honest – make you happy and fill you with joy? Is it gloriously focused on the Lord Jesus Christ?

Truth matters

Jesus said, 'Consider carefully what you hear' and 'how you listen' (Mark 4:24; Luke 8:18). His words are a perfect heading for Deuteronomy 13. There are always false prophets and false teachers around (Matt. 24:23–25; 2 Thes. 2:9; 2 Pet. 2:1). Deuteronomy 13 raises up a salutary banner of warning and offers three typical situations.

In the first (vv. 1–5), the false teaching is backed by *the evidence of a 'sign or wonder'*, which is offered as supernatural 'proof' of the teaching. That is not the proper test, says Moses. All teaching must be tested by fundamental truth. Is what is taught consistent with the Lord's self-revelation at the exodus (v. 5)? The six verbs in verse 4 indicate the rigidity and firmness with which we are to hold and practise what the Lord has revealed and spoken.

The second typical situation (vv. 6–11) imposes a different and very searching test on us – *the pressure of people* we love urging on us beliefs and practices which contradict what the Lord revealed at the exodus (v. 10) What a severe test if to hold to the truth means losing family and friends! But if we go with our dear ones, we lose the truth (cf. Luke 14:26). Again, the requirement is to test all teaching by fundamental truth.

Moses has a third example to offer (vv. 12–17): *the insidious attraction of popularity*, going with the crowd and doing what 'everyone is doing'. Here is a whole city going after false doctrine, enabling its advocates to apply the pressure by arguing, 'But everyone believes it'. It is not always easy to stand out from the crowd, is it? Yet we must stand up and be counted.

When we read of the penalty to be imposed on the false teachers (vv. 5, 9–10, 15–16), please let not our first reaction be horror. The penalties were for then, and as far as we are concerned they are intended to make us aware of the frightful seriousness of the error involved – departing from basic revelation. All these penalties are what this sin merits. How intent, then, we should be to steer clear of it, instead following through verse 4 and the concluding summary verse 18. Hold to the word of God.

REFLECTION

Consider how we too are urged, 'Test everything. Hold on to the good' (1 Thes. 5:21).

READ Deuteronomy 14:1–29

The Lord's children: mourning, eating, sharing and caring

True to the whole of Scripture, the rules, regulations and practices from Deuteronomy 14:1 to 26:19 are not given so that we may 'become' God's children, but because we 'are'. 1:31 and 8:5 speak of the same relationship but from the Father's point of view – how he cares for and educates his children. Now the issue is how the members of the divine family behave, and, again typically of the Bible, the directions start with the ordinary and the humdrum – a death in the family (v. 1); what happens in the kitchen and is stored in the pantry (vv. 3–21); and handling the family income (vv. 22–29). It is in these everyday, down-to-earth things that the difference of God's people is to be evident. Great issues are faced in unspectacular situations.

Bodily disfigurement was standard pagan mourning practice (see Is. 15:2; 22:12; Jer. 16:6; Ezek. 7:18), though it is not explained. Yet God's children (Deut. 14:1) are 'holy' (v. 2) and defined as '[belonging] to the LORD' – essentially they are living within a different environment and partakers of a different arena of life, not just negatively different from the surrounding world but positively so, as a 'treasured possession'. Paul caught the whole idea here when he counselled not sorrowing as others who have no hope (1 Thes. 4:13).

The food permissions and restrictions (Deut. 14:3–21; cf. Mark 7:19) are also unexplained. The great old Brethren writer, C.H. Mackintosh, found symbolism where possible and explained chewing the cud as proper inward digestion, and parting or splitting the hoof as leaving the correct footprint – so that the 'clean' beasts reflected the believer's task of digesting and living out divine truth. The explanation is delightful but hard to apply to birds and fish. Rather, we are firmly cautioned that our lifestyle matters.

Deuteronomy has a lovely extension to the tithe laws (Lev. 27:30–33; Num. 18:21–29), making the regular tithe an occasion for a family feast with invited guests (Deut. 14:26–27), and adding the special third-year tithe (v. 28) as a local, social provision for the needy. It all adds up to being different by being your true self.

REFLECTION

Christians have a distinctive 'national dress'. As Paul urges in Romans 13:14, 'clothe yourselves with the Lord Jesus Christ' – 'Lord' by obeying, 'Jesus' by imitating his lovely life, and 'Christ' by resting on his finished work of salvation.

DAY 21

READ Deuteronomy 15:1–23

One God, one society

Moses now turns his attention to people who fall into debt (vv. 1–6), the poor who need sustaining (vv. 7–11) and those who hire themselves out in service (vv. 12–18). The basic truth he asserts is that since there is only one God, there must also be only one society.

Every seventh year called for the wiping of the debtor's slate clean. It was called 'the LORD's time for cancelling debts' (v. 2). In other words, the Israelites must do this because God is like that; the way he deals with us is the model for our dealing with each other. There are to be no half measures; the whole debt is to be cleared away by remission. It is to be all gone, just like our sins.

What would be the equivalent today? Probably, where possible, making gifts, not loans; or where possible translating loans into gifts – and forgetting about them. This would be radical indeed in a society which worships 'market forces', would it not? But it is the way the Lord's market 'works' (v. 6) – and the way to come out economically on top!

In case we miss the message, it is repeated in verses 7–11. See how they are inside the bracket of the tight fist (v. 7) and the open hand (v. 11) – and not a grudging hand at that but one which matches the open heart (v. 8).

The third area in which we are called to model ourselves on divine action is in an understanding, generous treatment of servants (vv. 12–18). It speaks loudly of the sort of society Moses envisaged that he felt he had to legislate specifically for the servant who did not want his service terminated (vv. 16–17)! But the essence again is to act as the Lord has acted for us (v. 15). It is the same high and holy standard throughout: my calling is to be to everyone else what the Lord is to me. As someone wrote, 'And from your eyes he beckons me, and from your heart his love is shed – till I lose sight of you and see the Christ instead.'[3]

In the light of all this, the final verses (19–23) are right within context. Using the rules for the firstborn as a case in point, the ordinances the Lord has appointed serve to keep our eyes on him whom we are to copy, to bring him right into our lives all the time, and especially to remind us – by focusing on the firstborn – of the great redemption in and from Egypt when the Lord redeemed his firstborn son (Ex. 4:22; 12:25–27).

REFLECTION

We must treat others mindful of how God has treated us (Eph. 4:32; Col. 3:12–13; 1 Pet. 2:20–25; 3:8–9).

DAY 22

READ Deuteronomy 16:1–17

'Thy Presence makes the feast'

When Charles Wesley sang, 'Thy Presence makes the Feast,'[4] he might well have derived the thought from Deuteronomy 16. Out of all the feasts of the Lord (cf. Lev. 23), Moses concentrated on the great trio of those of the Passover, Weeks and Tabernacles, uniting them round the common demand that they be celebrated at the place the Lord chooses (vv. 2, 6, 7, 11, 15, 16).

Particularly, perhaps, in the case of the Passover, which at its foundational celebration was totally domestic (Ex. 12), there might have been a tendency, in Canaan, to keep the feast at home. According to Moses, though, obedience is at stake: the Lord has a chosen place; do as he says. In the sterling words of John Calvin, 'Worship must be conformable to the will of God as its unerring standard.' And only at the chosen place was there a guarantee of divine presence – his name is there (Deut. 16:2, 6, 11). Surely this should be our central concern – the contentment of the Lord to be among us, and the abhorrence and banishment of anything in us individually or collectively that is offensive to his holy presence. Is not this why Scripture calls us to self-examination before coming to the Lord's Supper (1 Cor. 11:28)?

This central trio of feasts offers a pictorial view of the focal points of worship. Passover (Deut. 16:1–8) looks back to our once-for-all redemption. The Feast of Weeks (vv. 9–12) rejoices in the present gifts of God – its New Testament emphasis rests on the gift of the Holy Spirit, its Old Testament emphasis rested on the gift of the law (cf. v. 12). As to the Feast of Tabernacles (vv. 13–15), Deuteronomy overlooks the requirement to live in ramshackle 'booths' (Lev. 23:40–42) – a recollection of wilderness vulnerability, divine provision, safety and safe homecoming – but its timing underlines consummation, with the harvest home and 'gathered' (Deut. 16:13). It makes us look forward to the Second Coming and the final great gathering of the whole redeemed people.

REFLECTION

The scroll the Lamb holds in his hand (Rev. 5:6–7) is the book of life (Rev. 21:27): the list of all who have been redeemed by his blood; given to the Son by the Father (John 6:39–40); who rejoice that their names are written in heaven (Luke 10:20); his elect for whom he will one day send out his angels (Mark 13:27); and those who will meet him in the air when he comes again (1 Thes. 4:17).

DAY 23 **READ** Deuteronomy 16:18 – 17:20

Leadership, part 1: *Judges, priests and kings*

There was nothing special about the leaders of Israel – any more than there is anything special required by the leadership qualifications in 1 Timothy 3:1–13 and Titus 1:5–9. Leaders are just to be 'Exhibit A' of what it means to be a member of the redeemed people.

In connection with judges (Deut. 16:18–20), notice how what 'they' must be (v. 18) turns into what 'you' must be (vv. 19-20)! 16:21 – 17:8 look intrusive on a more personal level. There is a sudden change of topic from just judges to religious integrity. We shall see the same sudden change in 18:8–13. It's the way Deuteronomy works. Life is all one piece. There are no special compartments – one for the courts, another for religion; one for judges, another for priests. Life is one, and we are called to be people of proved integrity everywhere – totally devoted to principles and practices of righteousness and justice, and totally committed to the sole worship of one, only God.

But though we are all on the same level in our submission to the justice and worship of the Lord, Deuteronomy does not subscribe to a situation of 'all chiefs, no Indians'. The judges and priests are God's intended leaders, and are there to be obeyed. As in the New Testament, there is no such thing as a church without leaders, yet it is essential that these leaders be subject to what the Lord has revealed and commanded. And the same applies to the envisaged king (vv. 14–20), who also – and marvellously – pictures what you and I would wish to be. He does not confuse greatness with force (v. 16); he carefully avoids entanglements that foreseeably would distract his heart from the Lord (v. 17a, cf. 1 Kgs 11:1–4); he is not covetous for wealth (v. 17b); he is a man of the word of God – devoted to it to the smallest detail (v. 18), treasuring it as a personal possession (v. 19a), and an assiduous reader of it (v. 19b), knowing that this would keep his relationships right (v. 20a), hold him to the life of obedience (v. 20b) and prosper his reign and his family (v. 20c). Will not the word of God do the same for us?

REFLECTION

Reading this passage should stimulate us to a greater concern for those who lead us in church and society – and our solemn duty to pray constantly for them. Beware of the motto, 'Why pray when you can criticise'!

DAY 24

READ Deuteronomy 18:1–22

Leadership, part 2: *priests, Levites and prophets*

We need to think very carefully about 'priests' in the Old Testament. It is important to remember that they were an interim arrangement until such time as the Lord's ideal could happen – a whole nation of priests (Ex. 19:4–6). This was fulfilled in the New Testament (1 Pet. 2:9). Consequently, in the New Testament the word 'priest' is only used in two ways: in the singular, it refers to the Lord Jesus Christ (see Heb. 6:20); and in the plural, to all Christian people, the priesthood of all believers (see Rev. 1:6; 5:10). There is no such thing in the New Testament Church (nor should there be in any church today) of a separate order of 'priests'. Jesus is our great High Priest, and we are his under-priests, with access through him within 'the curtain' (Heb. 10:19–22) – or, as Deuteronomy 18:5 says, 'to stand and minister in the LORD's name always'.

While verses 1–8 speak to us mainly in terms of our privileged position, verses 9–14 speak in terms of direct warning and prohibition. Like today's world with its horoscopes, the ancient world was full of claimants to foretell the future – by all sorts of means (see Ezek. 21:21), including communication with the dead (v. 11). The Lord calls both the practices (v. 9) and the practitioners (v. 12) 'detestable', and puts such exercises on the same level as the human sacrifice by fire of sons and daughters (v. 10). It is all a corrupt attempt to gain control of our future. Don't do it! Rest content with the prophetic word of God (vv. 15–22).

The question arises, however, of how we are to relate what is promised here (a great prophet, like Moses) with what actually happened (a whole line of prophets). Just put yourself in the position of an ancient Israelite, and all is clear: when a prophet arises you ask the question, 'Is this the promised prophet like Moses?' (see John 1:21). The same would happen in relation to the successive kings of David's line: 'Is this the promised Messianic King?' The New Testament is the Old Testament brought to completion; Jesus is the desire of all nations and he has come.

REFLECTION

Rejoice in this great truth: 'Peace, perfect peace, our future all unknown? Jesus we know, and He is on the throne!'[5]

DAY 25

READ Deuteronomy 19:1–21

Safeguarding

Six times in this chapter (vv.1, 2, 3, 8, 10, 14) Moses reminds his hearers that they are going to live in the land the Lord will give – the land he has planned for them. What a sense of *divine providence* that was meant to give them! Rainfall, fruitfulness, peace, prospering – all are his plan and gift; drought, barrenness, attack, want – all are under his control and direction! But is he not equally Lord of *our* circumstances? And should we not have the same sense of obligation to live responsively?

In chapter 19 this response is stated in terms of *integrity within the law*: people must be protected from undeserved penalty (vv. 4–7); from mistaken leniency (vv. 11–13); from underhand malpractice (v. 14); and from malicious accusation (vv. 15–20). Old Testament law had a great concern to protect people, and the provision of cities of refuge is a good example. They understood degrees of murder. Manslaughter is clearly defined (vv. 4–6), and refuge is made accessible ('centrally located', v. 2), attainable ('build roads to them', v. 3) and assured (to 'save his life', v. 5).

The introduction of land inheritance (v. 14) may seem unexpected here, but it shows what a serious offence tampering with the Lord's allocation was considered to be (cf. Josh. 14; 1 Kgs 21:3). Furthermore, in a rather free-flowing spoken word like this part of Deuteronomy is (chapters 19–25 are a loosely connected development of commandments 6–10), Moses links two 'sneaky' offences – changing boundaries and false charge. The 'sneak' is to be 'rewarded' by paying the penalty he thought to inflict (v. 19).

This principle lies behind most of the imprecations in the psalms (see Ps. 109:14–20) – the curses are not vindictive plans for personal action, nor should they even be assumed to be matched by vindictive feelings on the part of the psalmist; they are prayers that the Lord will impose the outcome of false accusation on the false accuser. True prayers leave justice to God. Neither is the summarising verse 21 a recipe for unbridled savagery, but a law of absolute equality: *the punishment must match the crime exactly, no less and no more!* It does not specify a punishment to be inflicted, but a principle of strict equality in sentencing.

REFLECTION

In Matthew 5:38–42 the Lord Jesus took issue with some who were making a principle intended to guide a judge in passing sentence into a policy of retaliation in private quarrels.

READ Deuteronomy 20:1–20

War is a holy thing

If David had read Deuteronomy as 17:18–20 directed, he would never have made war as he did, led astray by unthinking 'kingly' logic – 'am king, have army, will fight'. Chapter 20 has in mind the wars of occupation of the Promised Land. David was indeed the best of the kings and a standard the remainder rarely achieved, but where, for example, was the voice of the Lord directing him to war against the pathetic scrap of the house of Saul (2 Sam. 3:6)? What justified him in attacking Hadadezer just because his back was turned and he was preoccupied elsewhere (2 Sam. 8:3; Ps. 60)?

According to Deuteronomy 20, first, war must be specifically and divinely authorised (vv. 1–4). The priest calls the people to war and accompanies the call with the assurance that the mighty God of the Exodus guarantees victory (vv. 1, 4). Their confidence is not the hollow piety of politicians who trumpet 'the justness of our cause' and 'the help of Almighty God', but the assurance that this is the Lord's war before it is theirs.

Secondly, considerations of humanity take pride of place above 'the war effort' (vv. 5–9) – with regard for the enjoyment of property (v. 5), land (v. 6) and marriage (v. 7), and discharge papers for all those for whom military service would be an intolerable burden (v. 8). How very far this is from the sentiment that the only way to fight a war is to hit the enemy with every weapon to hand! It is also far from the oft-repeated mantra of the 1940s, 'Don't you know there's a war on?', and its justification for every intrusive, thoughtless inhumanity!

Thirdly, in verses 10–20, Deuteronomy turns to rules of engagement – the priority of peacemaking (v. 11); discriminatory action against those who will not make peace (vv. 12–14); and the difference between foes afar and foes near (vv. 15–18). When we find ourselves revolted by the 'completely destroy' edict of verse 17, we need to ask if we share the Bible's view of the horror of false religion and its influences. For while we would not imitate the practice (cf. 1 Kgs 18:40), we are called to share the revulsion.

Finally, in verses 19–20, think of the wilderness desolations of First World War battlefields, or the burnt-out shells of Coventry or Dresden, and compare this with the ecologically sensitive requirements of verses 19–20.

REFLECTION

The armour Christians wear is the armour of the Gospel to engage in the war of the Gospel (Eph. 6:10–18; 1 Thes. 5:8).

DAY 27

READ Deuteronomy 21:1–23

The protection of the law

There are five sections in this chapter (vv. 1–9; 10–14; 15–17; 18–21; and 22–23). The three middle sections are linked like dominoes, that is, by matching topics: a second wife (vv. 10–14); the son of a second wife treated unfairly by a parent (vv. 15–17); and a son who is a menace to his parents (vv. 18–21). The first and last parts share a reference to the land as a divine gift (vv. 1, 23), and the need to cleanse the land (vv. 9, 23). The great linking thought of all five is that the law is intended for protection – and it is in this way the passage speaks to us, not least that we should pray for our laws and our lawmakers.

First, *the law should protect the vulnerable from the strong* (vv. 10–14). We desperately need this aspect of law in a day when post-victory rape is far from discouraged. Here the girl who is 'fancied' is treated as a person in her own right, with respect and restraint, and with the status and protection of marriage.

Secondly, *the law should guarantee the rights of the potentially defrauded* (vv. 15–17) – in this case the son of the less-loved wife and his rights as firstborn.

Thirdly, *the law should take the side of parents in despair over a child out of control* (vv. 18–21). See how the Old Testament does not give absolute right to a father to do as he pleases in his family. The law steps in. There is no recorded case where the rigour of this regulation was applied. However, it is very likely the appearance of the wilful son in court and the threatened penalty was meant itself to produce the desired reformation.

Fourthly, *the law should safeguard the land itself from pollution* (vv. 22–23). We are not familiar with this idea of our sin defiling the land we live in, but it is stressed in the Bible (see Jer. 3:1), and goes back to Genesis 3:17–19. Indeed, the land thus defiled becomes an active force opposing its inhabitants (see Lev. 18:25). Our greatest environmental contribution is our holiness. Thus the crime leading to the unsolved murder must not be left without 'atonement' (Deut. 21:8) – the word means 'covering', not is the sense of hiding (sweeping under the carpet) but as the payment of the price that 'covers' a debt. The exposure of the body after execution (v. 23), leaving what is a curse to God displayed, is a defilement. The land is his gift and is itself a holy thing.

REFLECTION

In what ways can we apply each of the above points to ourselves and to today's world? How can we bring home such significant truths to our leaders?

DAY 28

READ Deuteronomy 22:1–30

Purging the community

At first sight chapter 22 is just a mixum-gatherum of assorted bits and pieces, some of which have a loose link with the seventh commandment. Closer examination suggests that the theme is purging society (as is explicit in vv. 21, 22, 24).

Moses opens with brotherliness (vv. 1–4). Contrary to the tendency not to get involved, we must accept a responsibility of care for each other. Note how 'your brother' (vv. 1, 4) brackets the verses. You may not know him or he may be at the other end of the country (v. 2), but he is still 'your brother'.

The word 'detests' (v. 5; 'abomination', NKJV) suggests some foul religious element in cross-dressing. The distinction of the sexes is sacred to the Lord. In the next example, where the principle of immediate advantage says take the eggs and the mature bird found (vv. 6–7), the ongoing security of the community ('long life', v. 7) means our actions must take a longer view. Likewise, immediate advantage suggests avoiding the expense of adding a parapet to the roof (v. 8); care for the community says otherwise. Verses 9–11 offer no explanation, and may be best left at that! On the other hand, reference to Leviticus 19:19 suggests a call to respect the order and ordering of creation – each seed has its proper place, each animal its proper work, and each person should show in dress an avoidance of compromise. The stress in verse 12 is lost in translation – it is 'the covering with which you are covered'. Nakedness was a feature of pagan, orgiastic worship; in a way that is not clear, the provision of 'tassels' was an extra guarantee of modesty and seemliness.

One thread binds verses 13–29: marriage and sex belong inseparably together in a pure society. Do we flinch at the harshness of the death penalty (vv. 21, 24)? Of course we do – but it is in part because we no longer class adultery and fornication as 'serious'. Balance that severity, however, with the humanitarian insistence that the misused girl be taken in an indissoluble marriage (vv. 19, 29). That is not a great start to home life, we would say. No, but it is providing shelter and provision for one who would otherwise be an unmarriageable outcast. The Lord's laws are marvellously caring towards the vulnerable – as all true laws should be – of which the 'benefit of the doubt' regulation of verses 25–27 is a striking example.

REFLECTION

Pray for our legislators. Pray for humane, considerate laws. Get involved in creating a caring, pure community.

Monday as well as Sunday

Read the amazing Leviticus 19 and learn – as is true of all Old Testament Law – that the Lord has a word for us, a way of life for every situation and relationship. Biblical religion cannot be boxed in.

So in Deuteronomy 23, side by side, without any sense of impropriety, we have Israel focused on the inmost sacredness of religion (vv. 1–8), and Israel concerned with toilet arrangements in the camp (vv. 9–14), humanitarianism (vv. 15–16), financial purity (vv. 17–18), brotherliness (vv. 19–20), personal reliability (vv. 21–23) and integrity of ownership (vv. 24–25). In a word, Sunday's worship and Monday's needs, tasks and relationships are all of a piece. The two focal points of the Decalogue (commandments 1–4 and 5–10) make the same point. We need to beware of praying on our knees on Sunday and preying on our neighbours for the rest of the week!

The purity of the assembly is important (vv. 1–8). First, as regards the corrupting influence of false religion: verses 1–2 are concerned with unholy rituals (v. 1) and illicit relationships (v. 2). Secondly, the Bible does not subscribe to the view that every religion makes a contribution to the sum total of truth: there has to be a godly principle of separation (vv. 3–6). Thirdly, we may smile at the thought of the Lord being offended by our sanitary arrangements, but there is a requirement of everything to be decent and in order, and we need to be reminded that this applies more widely than just to what happens in the pew.

Verses 17–18 need understanding. The two categories of persons mentioned are, literally, 'holy' women and 'holy' men, where 'holy' means separated off for service to their god – a 'service' which, in Baal worship, meant engaging in sexual activities. Such 'worship' Baal required, but, to the Lord God, it was an abhorrent equivalent to prostitution. Bringing in a fee (v. 18) must refer to income earned in the course of Baal service, and is true to the Bible's view of money: what matters is how it was gained and how it is used.

REFLECTION

Jesus teaches us what is true wealth (Luke 12:21; Matt.6:33) and the correct attitude toward possessions (Acts 2:44–47; 4:32–34).

READ Deuteronomy 24:1–22

People are people, not commodities

There is at least one thread running through chapter 24: people must be treated as persons in their own right, not as a means to someone else's profit. A pledge taken to guarantee a loan must study humanity, and the debtor's human needs met (vv. 6, 10–13). Kidnapping (v. 7) – presumably to sell as a slave or to hold to ransom (today it would be called 'human trafficking') – commands the death penalty. Wages must be fair (v. 14) and payment regular and prompt (v. 15). The vulnerable (refugees, orphans and widows) are a charge on those with resources (vv. 17–22).

People are also to be treated as personally responsible: in a case of infectious uncleanness (v. 8) and regarding sin committed (v. 16) the person must accept the consequences. This is what the Lord made Miriam do (v.9; cf. Num. 12:9, 10, 15). It is the price of being a human person.

Underlying all this ordering of society, there are principles: we are to be directed by the word and acts of God (vv. 8–9); we are to act towards others as God has acted towards us (vv. 18, 22); and we are to live in relationship to others aware of the watchful eye of God (vv. 13, 15, 19).

The regulations for marriage, divorce and remarriage (vv. 1–4) are full of unexplained detail: what caused the original divorce? It says 'a nakedness of a matter' (v.1, literally), an expression used in 23:14 of falling below pubic seemliness – possibly here even pointing to something vague like 'for some acceptable cause'. Nor do we know what caused the 'dislike' (v. 3) leading to the second divorce. Nor, finally, is the charge of defilement (v. 4) explained. We can but assume that so much is left unexplained because Deuteronomy wants only to make the substantial point of the impossibility of re-establishing the first marriage. It is clear, then, that there is no objection to remarriage after divorce. Indeed it seems to be assumed that the divorced wife will remarry – and, come to that, should she wish to remarry a second time, this would apparently be acceptable. What is impossible is a renewal of the first marriage. This is all the Old Testament ever says about divorce and remarriage.

REFLECTION

There is a better way than divorce (Mal. 2:13–16; 1 Cor. 7:10–16).

The disadvantaged command our concern

Would it not be easy to come to this chapter and groan inwardly? More laws! How we need to remind ourselves that all this too is the word of God! A particular law may reflect a bygone society; it may suggest an inapplicable procedure; but it is still intended as a vehicle of divine truth; it still speaks to direct us.

The guilty party at court (vv. 1–3), for example, must be allowed due process of law (v. 1a); sentence must be by those authorised to pronounce sentence (v. 1b); and punishment must be under supervision (v. 2a), must be appropriate to the crime (v. 2b), and must not be dishonouring or degrading (v. 3).

The regulation about oxen (v. 4) is one we do not expect here, but that does not mean it is out of place or misplaced by some clownish editor. No, it is among its companion laws to make us see how important it is in the eyes of God. Our animals are always capable of being disadvantaged; it matters how we treat them.

Brothers-in-law may well be grateful that verses 5–10 do not apply today! But the principle does apply: widows are our care, especially those in our own families (see 1 Tim. 5:8, 16).

The law about the intervening wife (vv. 11–12) is, of course, here to warn us that not every intervention on behalf of the disadvantaged is allowable. The sentence (v. 12) is the only case of penalty by mutilation in the Old Testament, and, very likely, the existence of this law would have guaranteed by itself that it would never need to be carried out! It does imply, however, that some greater offence than immodesty must be in mind. For example, perhaps the man was so injured in his private parts that he became infertile. Speculation, however, takes us nowhere. We are simply warned that intervention on behalf of those we see as disadvantaged must be thoughtful, appropriate and controlled.

Customers can be at the mercy of shopkeepers (vv. 13–16)! Perfect weights and exact measures are a safeguard against selling underweight for overprice.

In verses 17–19 there is another example of inappropriate action against the disadvantaged. The Amalekites' attack was against the Israelite stragglers, who were tired and weary (v. 18) – presumably the slow, the elderly and the disabled. In the sight of the Lord this was a capital offence, and a warning regarding every interventionist act of war.

REFLECTION

In Matthew 26:51–54 Peter's intended action fell well within the 'rules' of a just war (as it is now called). Jesus would have none of it.

DAY 32

READ Deuteronomy 26:1–19

Making confession

Note how entering the land (v. 1) matches the same thought in 12:1; and how the reference to 'the place that the LORD your God will choose' (26:2) forms a bracket with 12:5. In this way 26:1–19 rounds off Moses' extended review of the Decalogue which 12:1 began. Old Testament religion is not just a matter of obeying rules and observing ceremonies. Behind it all lies personal conviction, testimony to salvation and commitment to obedience.

In verses 1–11 the individual worshipper identifies himself with the salvation history of the Lord's people (note 'us ... we ... our ...' in vv. 6–9). He makes this testimony his own in verses 13–14 (note 'I' throughout). Finally, in verses 17–19 Moses affirms the resultant position (note 'you' throughout): first what they have in principle affirmed of the Lord, and then what he affirms of them.

The occasions are significant. The offering of firstfruits (vv. 1–11) would seal their occupation and enjoyment of the land; the offering of the tithe (vv. 12–14) would mark the completion of the first three-year period of inheritance. Joyful inheritance and assured possession of what the Lord promised were marked by personal testimony and renewed commitment.

The testimony begins with dire need. We can translate either/both 'wandering' (v. 5, NIV) or 'ready to perish' (v. 5, NKJV) as a situation of no hope if left to oneself. Next came actual danger of death (v. 6) under a cruel master – they were crushed ('ill-treated') and their life was burdened with trouble ('labour') against overwhelming odds ('oppression', v. 7). From all of this it was not any effort or ability of their own that saved them but the Lord's open ear (v. 7), plus his hand of intervention and his arm of strength (v. 8).

All of this is precisely the testimony we would give of our salvation in Christ. And the Lord's desires for those whom he has saved remain the same: strictly performed obedience, particularly care for the needy (vv. 13–14). Life lived in conformity to his statutes by those who listen to his word (v. 17, where 'obey' is 'listen to') is the outstanding mark of his 'treasured possession' (v. 18), and this is the key to blessing (v. 19). We do not obey in order to become special, but because we are! Seeking blessing through obedience is not turning to salvation by works, but recognising that obedience is a means of grace for those who are saved (see Acts 5:32).

REFLECTION

Look at John 14:15–16 and trace the sequence: exhibiting proof of love leads to receiving means of grace (cf. 14:21, 23).

DAY 33

READ Deuteronomy 27:1–26

Our permanent address

If you read straight from 26:19 to 28:1 you will begin to think of chapter 27 as an intruder. Nevertheless it is exactly in place! First, because it links with 11:26–32 in forming part of the 'frame' around Moses' great meditation on the Ten Commandments (12:1 - 26:19), but also because it has something important to say in its own right before we can fully appreciate the seriousness of the blessings and curses of chapters 28–29.

When Israel entered the Promised Land they were directed to make God's word part of the very fabric of the land given to them (27:1–4). They were to identify Mounts Gerizim and Ebal (vv. 12–13) as at the centre of their new homeland, and remember the two sides of the covenant the Lord made with them: its blessings (for the obedient, 28:1–14) and its curses (on the disobedient, 27:15–26). The centrality of God's revealed word was not a 'take-it-or-leave-it' option; it was the fabric of life. This is what it means to be the Lord's people, says verse 9: the day they 'became' his people was the day they set up the stones on the mounts. When we become Christians, we come inescapably within the embrace of Holy Scripture.

But something else was set up also. On Mount Ebal - the mount of the curses - they were directed to build the Lord's altar (vv. 4–7). They not only lived under the rule of God's word but, as Paul puts it, 'where sin increased, grace increased all the more' (Rom. 5:20). The Lord who calls us to obedience and consequent blessing knows our weakness, and positions his altar of mercy to coincide with our sin, failure and merited condemnation. Where we fail we can also recommit (the burnt offering, v. 6, symbolises 'holding nothing back', cf. Gen. 22:12), find atonement (Lev. 1:4) and re-enter divine fellowship (through fellowship offerings, v. 7). Like genuine silver and gold bear a hallmark, so the people of God advertise their genuineness by obeying (literally, listening to and heeding) and observing his word (v. 10).

REFLECTION

2 Timothy 3:14 calls us to 'continue' in what we have learned - all that we've been taught is to take up permanent residence within us. This encompasses, on the one hand, all of Paul's apostolic teaching, representing the New Testament ('my teaching', 3:10), and on the other hand, the Old Testament in which Paul had been instructed since infancy ('holy Scriptures', 3:14).

Inheriting blessing

Verse 8 lies at the centre of three concentric circles. In itself it is the Lord's pledge of blessing for his people.

The outer circle (vv. 1–2, 13–14) says that the Lord will exalt his people 'if' they obey his voice (v. 1) and 'because' they listen to his commands (v.13, literally). It is not a matter of obeying just this command or that, but of obeying all his commands. For this reason we are not involved in a 'slot machine' situation whereby we put in our sixpenny worth of obedience and demand sixpenny worth of blessing. Our obedience is always imperfect; if the Lord chooses to bless us, it is wholly of his grace. Nevertheless, by serious, devoted obedience and by listening to his word we can, so to say, put ourselves in the way of blessing. Obedience is a means of grace.

The next circle (vv. 3–5, 11–12) reveals the Lord as being directly involved in every area of our lives, whether we think of the family, the farm or the pantry (vv. 3–5); whether it is a matter of having children and profiting agriculturally (v. 11), or needing rain or doing well at work (v. 12). That is to say, every area is within the scope of the call to obey and listen. The word of God is the constant accompaniment of life.

The inner circle places us in relation to other people (vv. 6–7, 9–10). In verse 6 we are involved in the comings and goings of life; verse 7 directly concerns Moses' hearers as a nation among nations and promises security against attack. The legitimate equivalent today is the 'warfare' of the Gospel, and the effectiveness of evangelism. But, according to the balancing verses (9–10), victory is not a matter in the past of weaponry and today of method, but of holiness (v. 9) and the distinctiveness of bearing the Lord's name (v. 10).

Throughout there is a total identification of the Lord with his word. Where it is, he is; where we turn aside from his word, we turn aside from him to other gods (v. 14). According to verse 2, which the NKJV renders as, 'And all these blessings shall come upon you and overtake you, because you obey the voice of the Lord your God', we are involved in a race, with God's blessing playing catch up. When we turn from his word, the distance opens up; when we tarry with his word, his blessing overtakes us!

REFLECTION

Consider this counsel:
'Take time to be holy;
speak oft with thy Lord.
Abide in him always and
feed on his word.'[6]

Blight

Today's passage makes grim reading, but brings a message that must not be overlooked. It spells out in detail what other Bible writers, so to say, sketch in. Note the significant 'therefore' in Amos 3:2 – the privilege of being known by the Lord brings the inevitability of punishment. To whom much is given, from him much will be required (Luke 12:48). Leviticus 26:25 uses the telling phase 'to avenge the breaking of the covenant' – an inbuilt reaction to disobedience within God's gracious relationship with his people. The verses in Deuteronomy 28 leave no stone unturned to bring this message home to us.

Disobedience (v. 15) casts a blight over the whole of life. Verses 16–19 show the contrast with the life of obedience and blessing (28:4–6). Verses 20–24 are a chorus of punishment until Israel is destroyed or perishes (vv. 20, 21, 22, 24) – disobedience is a total destroyer (vv. 23–24, cf. vv. 38–42). This brings up the question of environmental consequences. Biblically speaking, the creation is always on the side of the Creator, and reflects the relationship of sinners to the holy God. Hence, for example, in Genesis 3:17–19, the 'thorns and thistles' and the increased problems of extracting a living from the soil. This is seen even more violently in Leviticus 18:25. Deuteronomy 28:27–35 are bracketed by a reference to boils and the caution about diseases that cannot be healed, and in the middle is a cloud of frustration, disaster and disappointment that overshadows the disobedient.

Just as we noted yesterday that there is a symbolic relationship between the Lord and his word, so that rejecting it is rejecting him, so there is a symbolic relationship between the Lord's people and his word, so that when we allow our lives to become out of kilter with the word of God, we are automatically out of sorts with the Lord himself and his mercies. Just as obedience is a means of grace, so disobedience is a means of blight. Biblically, it is far more serious to fall out of harmonious fellowship with God than it is to fall into the hands of Satan! Bringing forth the sour grapes of unrighteousness and disobedience lets the wild beasts in to trample the vineyard (Is. 5:1–7).

REFLECTION

If we please God, he will not leave us (John 8:29).

The lost inheritance

The theme of this last section of chapter 28 is invasion with suffering, defeat and loss of the land given by the Lord. Read verses 45–48 as an introduction, noting how verse 48 couples the invading enemy with personal sufferings. Verses 49–51 then take up the tale of enemy incursion. In verses 52–57 the horrible consequences of prolonged siege are spelt out, further amplified in verses 58–62. Verses 63–68 predict the sad blow of loss of the precious land. Finally 29:1 rounds off Moses' covenant speech.

In this way both great truths and a dire warning are brought vividly before us. The first great truth – and how great it is! – is that the Lord is sovereign God of all the earth; all the nations are his to command. He 'sends' (v. 48) and brings (v. 49; literally, 'raises up') nations to do his bidding. The expression 'raises up' suggests that not only their arrival, but also their ability to act as they are doing, is under the Lord's sway. He is not an ornamental but an executive sovereign.

This means, secondly, that history is under moral control with moral objectives. The arrival of the enemy was what Israel deserved. To see history like this is to accept in faith what is revealed and to respond to it. The world does not look like a system of moral excellence, does it? The movement of men and nations does not seem to conform to a just system of reward and punishment, does it? But this is what the Bible teaches and faith accepts. We can look out on the chaos which the world presents to us at any given moment and shout a biblical 'Nevertheless!' All is in his hands!

The warning is that though we can never lose our salvation, we can lose our inheritance – as Paul teaches in 1 Corinthians 3:11–17. The loss of the God-given land is a severe illustration of this. So what was the cause of such a loss? There were three aspects to it: first, failure to listen to God's word ('obey' in Deut. 28:45, 62 is, literally, 'hear and listen to'); secondly, a lapse in personal devotion and joyful service to the Lord (v. 47); and thirdly, neglect of the book in which God's word was recorded for their learning (v. 58). The people to whom divine revelation is granted are called to live by that revelation; the possession of 'the book' leaves them without excuse.

REFLECTION

Dwell on the beautiful wonder of God's word (Ps. 19:7–11; 1 Cor. 2:9–13).

DAY 37

READ Deuteronomy 29:2–15

Today's the day

With 29:2 we begin the third speech of Moses (29:2 - 30:20; cf. 1:1 - 4:43 and 4:44 - 28:68), which leads into the last details – the appointment of Joshua to succeed Moses (31:1–29), Moses' song (31:30 - 32:43) and the record of his death and his blessing of his people (32:44 - 34:12). This third speech is as good a summary of the whole book as could be planned.

Today's portion falls into two sections. First, there is a review of history (vv. 3–8), introduced by the words 'all that the LORD did' (v. 2). Secondly, verses 9–15, where the word 'today'/'this day' comes five times, call for an immediate response. Verses 2–9 are a précis of the longer historical review in Deuteronomy 1–3, which is itself a précis of the full account in Exodus and Numbers. History is important! Biblical faith is not theological speculation (cf. 2 Pet. 1:16). It rests on the revealed truth of God, confirmed and secured by the historical acts of God.

Moses highlights the truths of redemption (vv. 2–3), demonstrated by the exodus; providential care (vv. 5–6), demonstrated by the wilderness years; and power over all the power of the enemy (vv. 7–8), demonstrated by the defeat of Sihon and Og and possession of their lands. Each element of this history has a truth to urge on Israel: the Lord is wholly sovereign, even to the extent that true spiritual awareness can only be ours by his gift (see v. 4); we are, however, responsible for learning the truth taught by God's historical acts (v. 6b), and for listening to and absorbing what God has said (v. 9).

Verses 10–15 contain only one truth: God's word is a 'today word'; it leaves no 'wriggle room' nor permission to temporise (cf. Ps. 95:7d–8; Heb. 3:7). It concerns the whole community – every member (vv. 10–11). Our immediate obedience is our way into covenant blessings (v. 12), bringing with it assurance that the Lord has accepted and confirmed us by oath as his people. It applies for all time (vv. 14–15). Every day is the Lord's 'today', and 'today' is the day for the obedience to the word of God which his covenant requires.

REFLECTION

'Today'/'this day' comes over twenty times in Deuteronomy, making immediacy characteristic of both the Lord's dealings and our response. It calls for prompt continuance through obedience (4:4), covenant membership (5:3), revelation (5:24), blessings through obedience (6:24), obedience itself (11:8) and commitment (13:4).

DAY 38

READ Deuteronomy 29:16–29

Only one loyalty

In this middle section of Moses' third speech it is clear that he is focusing on the first and second commandments as the core of covenant law and life. Israel had indeed seen the worship of other nations (v. 16). Their brush with Moabite religion (Num. 25), for example, must have left a sore memory, and itself constituted a clarion call to sole devotion to Yahweh. We need to remind ourselves that the ancient 'god' Baal is by no means a dead letter today. The 'god' of prosperity – of how to succeed, be productive and get rich, with its pursuit of a high Gross National Product and personal bank balance – is fully active and well cultivated in the world!

Notice, though, how coolly Moses consigns all other religions to the realm of the 'detestable' (Deut. 29:17), a root bearing 'bitter poison' (v. 18). They are not a second source of truth, not a teacher to learn from and not a philosophy with its own quota to contribute to the universal pool of learning. They are 'abominations' (v. 17, NKJV). Far from finding accommodation alongside the God of Israel in a homely syncretism, they cause turning 'away from the LORD' (v. 18). The call to sole loyalty and exclusive devotion to God, in religious exclusivism, is total.

This theme is taken a stage further in verses 22–29. Defection from the Lord is in every sense a killer (vv. 22–23) – not something met with divine understanding, tolerance, leniency and acceptance, but by 'fierce, burning anger' (v. 24), reminiscent of the insistence of the second commandment that the Lord is 'a jealous God' (Ex. 20:4). Defection is all the more inexcusable in that the life of loyalty is not a matter of guesswork or speculation. The Lord has written a book (Deut. 29:20–21, 27), making his truth readily available (cf. 30:14), and he summons his people to be people of that book.

This is the meaning of the great verse 29. It is easy to imagine some clever clogs in Israel being attracted to this or that pagan 'truth' and even congratulating himself (v. 19) – that he has penetrated deeper into things than his contemporaries, which is the attraction of a secret, esoteric religion. No, says verse 29. Leave secrets to God; your obligation is to what has been revealed. Make that enough for you.

REFLECTION

Treasure God's word, as this hymn does: 'The Church from her dear Master received the gift divine, and still that light she lifteth o'er all the earth to shine ... It is the chart and compass that o'er life's surging sea, mid mists and rocks and quicksands, still guides, O Christ, to Thee.'[7]

READ Deuteronomy 30:1–20

The wonder of repentance

This third section of Moses' speech, like the other two, is in two parts. In verses 1–10 he is probing the ultimate future, and in verses 11–20, challenging his people to a present choice. This is the way biblical prediction 'works'. The future is revealed not so that we can compose a calendar but so that we know how to live now.

As Moses sees it, the end is wonderful. The Lord is purposing to recover his people and bring them back to himself (v. 3), and he will do this when they repent (v. 2). Recalling the frightful sins and disasters of the last chapter, what a wonderful thing this repentance is. In response to repentance, the Lord reverses his own just retributions (v. 3); demonstrates his universal sway (v. 4); implements his promises (v. 5a); more than repeats the past (v. 5b); regenerates and renews individuals (v. 6); ends the oppression of the enemy (v. 7); and grants total prosperity (v. 9). Repentance, though, involves coming back to the Lord in loving devotion (vv. 2, 6, 20); obeying him (literally, 'listening to'/ 'heeding', vv. 2, 8, 10, 20); persevering in and keeping his commands (vv.10, 16); and a full, personal commitment, heart and soul (vv. 2, 6, 10). Penitent people are people of the book (v. 10).

The contrast between chapters 29 and 30 is itself an illustration of the truth Moses is preaching. The Israelites had departed from the Lord and found themselves walking in the pathways of death (29:22–28). They come to repentance and walk in the ways of life and prosperity (30:1–10). This prepares us for the resounding call of verses 11–20: now choose (v. 19)! We are suddenly back in the 'today' of 29:9–15. Since the future will demonstrate how wonderful repentance is in its simplicity and its results, should not the present be characterised by choosing life and eschewing the pathway of death? And this is all the more so since God's way is not the impossible path of salvation by works. We do not have to try to scale the heights or circle the globe (30:12–13). God has spoken (v. 14); our response is to walk with him in love (v. 20), and in the new life he inspires (v. 6).

REFLECTION

Psalm 51:3 opens with the word 'for', explaining how the blessings of verses 1–2 are ours. All that mercy, compassion and cleansing are ours, literally, 'because I acknowledge my transgressions'. That is the wonder of repentance.

DAY 40

READ Deuteronomy 31:1–29

Facing the future

We bid sad farewell to Moses in Deuteronomy 34, which makes chapters 31–33 his last words to us, with his thoughtful guidance for Israel's future. He starts by reminding them that fundamentally they are *a people of faith*. In verses 1–8, Israel is about to cross into the Promised Land. They and Joshua will need to summon up all the fortitude they can (vv. 6a, 7a). To enable them to do so, Moses simply points to the promises of God (vv. 3a, 6b, 8a) along with a reminder that the Lord has already signally kept his promises (v. 4) and can be relied on to do so again (v. 5).

Secondly, Moses reminds Israel that they are *people of the Book of the Law*. See how verses 9–29 are planned in an a-b-c-b-a formation: the book (vv. 9–13); Joshua commissioned (vv. 14–15); a cautioning against future defection (vv. 16–22); Joshua commissioned (v. 23); the book (vv. 24–29). As the Lord outlines the coming years through Moses, his people are firmly placed inside the bracket of the Book of the Law. This is their characteristic position. Recurringly it is the centrepiece of their worship gathering (vv. 10–11) – the simple reading of Holy Scripture – so that by listening they can learn, fear and follow (v. 12), and, by being exposed to Scripture, can be exposed to their own shortcomings (vv. 26, 28–29). The Feast of Tabernacles was a re-enactment of the vulnerable days in the wilderness when the Lord marvellously protected and provided for them (v. 10; cf. Lev. 23:42). Replicating that period, every seven years, they make themselves again, symbolically, the people with very little materially, but possessing the inestimable treasure of the word of God.

Finally, Moses urges Israel to be *a people fully self-aware* (vv. 16–21, 26–29). They are to be on their guard against complacency, knowing the sinfulness of their own hearts – how fickle (v. 16), rebellious (vv. 16, 20), corrupt (v. 29a) and provoking (v. 29b) they are. It is a sad but all too realistic catalogue.

REFLECTION

The reading of Scripture should still be the centre of worship – not the episodic, brief, perfunctory, badly read thing it too often is.

READ Deuteronomy 31:30 – 32:27

Facing life

The message of the Song of Moses is in the whole sweep of its poetry. He is seeking to make Israel face the meaning of their history and national experiences. So here we will not pick out particular truths, but try to 'take a stroll' through the first half of the song.

The appeal to listen in 32:1–2 is based, first, on who their God is (vv. 3–4) and then on their sad response (vv. 5–6). As 'Rock' he is steadfast and unchanging – especially in moral quality (v. 4b) but also in saving provision (Ex. 17:6), hence the Father who made you what you are (Deut. 32:6).

In the next section a retrospect starts with the organisation of the world around Israel (vv. 7–9). This is the meaning of 'according to the number of the sons of Israel' (v. 8). In appointing the nations their places, the Lord did so bearing in mind what his people, in their envisaged population, would need. In a word, they are central to his world rule, but also are the objects of his tender care (vv. 10–13). God found and safeguarded (v. 10), protected (v. 11), guided (v. 12) and settled Israel in their own land (vv. 13–14), with supernatural (v. 13) and natural (v. 14) provision.

But in verses 15–18, Israel's sad reaction of verse 5, in relation to what the Lord is known to be, is repeated – though in the face of the history of God's gracious dealing with them (vv. 7–14). The perils of prosperity (v. 15) led to disloyalty and provoking idolatry (vv. 16–17), with sinful forgetfulness (v. 18).

Now we see the Lord's reaction (vv. 19–22). He becomes jealous and angry (vv. 19–21a). The New Testament tells us that the means of provoking Israel to jealousy (v. 21) is the extension of the Gospel to Gentiles and their worldwide response to the offer of grace (Rom. 11:11–14). This suits the meaning here, of course, and prepares us for the message of world judgment in Deuteronomy 32:22, the assumption being (as is the case) that in every place the deepest divine anger would follow any rejection of the gospel message.

The final section today (vv. 23–27) notes the adversity that is inseparable from flouting the Lord's grace: divine alienation (v. 23), dislocation of the order of creation (v. 24), historical disaster (v. 25) but also divine forbearance prompted by anxiety lest his divine rule and prerogative be misunderstood and denied (v. 27).

REFLECTION

Romans 11:17–22 urges on us the task of making sure of our standing in the work of salvation (cf. 2 Peter 1:10).

Singing truth

Continuing our walk through Moses' Song, it is by no means easy to be sure how the remaining verses divide into sections. But taking our cue from two references to vengeance (vv. 35, 41), we can see that verses 28–33 bemoan the blindness of Israel to the work and ways of the Lord; verses 34–42 predict that the Lord will take up the case of his people; and verse 43 looks forward to universal jubilation.

In verses 28–33 a true wisdom would ponder the message of experience, and when the forces of the world triumph over the church, wisdom would know the reason why such a thing could happen. The answer is certainly not that our God has ceased to be 'the Rock', or that the pathetic 'rocks' of the world have suddenly become greater than the real Rock. Moses leaves the question hanging in the air. Even opponents would concede that it should not be so (v. 31); and on moral grounds the forces of the world cannot succeed, can they (vv. 32–33)? Are these not questions which cross the centuries to demand an answer today?

The only solution to an impotent church and a triumphalist world is that the God of vengeance should exert himself on our side (vv. 34–42). He has all the resources to do so (vv. 34–35), and Moses predicts that the Lord will take up the case of ('judge', v. 36) his people, out of pity for them, so, literally, noting our reduction to helplessness, and the dismal outcome of our false choices (vv. 37–38). How very marvellous! Where he has every right to condemn, he steps in to save – and he, and he alone, has the right and the power to do so (v. 39). He is on oath to do so (v. 40) and no action ever perpetrated against his people will go unobserved and unrequited (vv. 41–42).

The final twist in the story comes in verse 43: in his day of vengeance somehow (in ways Moses does not here describe) there will be an atonement in which his people will be joined with a worldwide gathering. Behind to 'make atonement' (v. 43) lies the verb 'to cover', not in the sense of hiding something out of sight, but in the same way as a sufficient price 'covers' and so cancels a debt.

REFLECTION

This hymn beautifully expresses the heart of Scripture regarding the coinciding of vengeance and atonement at the cross: 'In my place condemned he stood; sealed my pardon with his blood.'[8]

DAY 43

READ Deuteronomy 33:1–29

A grand farewell

It says everything about Moses' heart of love for his people that after all his travail with their cantankerous ways, and all the predicted dire consequences of their expected disobediences, his 'goodbye' is entirely one of warm well-wishing. Rightly it is called the 'blessing' of Moses.

The preface gives him the typical title of a prophet: 'man of God' (v. 1); and 34:10 proclaims him the prophetic supremo. Here he stands on the border of the Promised Land, which his heart aches to enter but cannot, and, letting his gaze sweep from the envisaged territory of Judah in the south (33:7) to Naphtali and Asher in the distant north (vv. 23–24), he pronounces his parting blessing. The thrust of the blessing is discernible as thus: the Lord has promised this land; his people by no means merit it; but divine promises are made to be kept, not broken, and kept they will be.

Did Reuben's heart fail when his name was mentioned (v. 6), thinking that, maybe, once again his awful sin would be given publicity (cf. Gen. 49:3–4). But no, this is a blessing; it is not an exposure of the past but a gentle wish for the future. Our sins are not forgotten, but neither are they ultimate barriers to the workings of grace.

Simeon is not listed – presumably Moses foresees his absorption into Judah, as actually happened (Josh. 19:1). Judah, though one of the most potent of the tribes, is reminded that inheritance is not by natural might or power but only by divine help (v. 7). Levi took his stand for God (Ex. 32:25–29; Num. 25:6–13) and learned that what grace enables grace also rewards. Levi became the guardian of the means of divine guidance (Deut. 33:8a; cf. Ex. 28:30; 1 Sam. 23:6–12), the teacher (v. 10a; cf. Mal. 2:4–7) and the priestly mediator (v. 10b). Benjamin was small among the tribes (Ps. 68:27) but would discover that even the welcoming love of his earthly father (Gen. 35:18) was surpassed by the close divine embrace (Deut. 33:12).

The blessing opens (vv. 1–5) and closes (vv. 26–29) by parallel statements balancing the Lord and his people. He comes to them at Sinai (v. 1) and they gather to him as their King (v. 5); he loves them and they bow at his feet (v. 3); he is the unique God (v. 26) and they are the unique people (v. 29). They are in his heart and hands (v. 3); they are in his shelter and his arms (v. 27).

REFLECTION

What blessings are promised to Joseph (vv. 13–17)? Why, in his case, is a reference to Exodus 3:1–8 especially appropriate (v. 16b)?

DAY 44

READ Deuteronomy 34:1–12

The best epitaph

Moses was not allowed a tomb suitable to his stature and record. He lies in an unmarked grave (v. 6). Had his grave been known, doubtless his body would have been exhumed and given what humans would have considered pride of place at the centre of the newly occupied land. But no, we too have to learn, with Moses, that what people might consider a minor slip (Num. 20:12) is totally major in the eyes of the Lord. Moses' entrance to the land would only come centuries later, and under the greatest of all auspices (Luke 9:30–31).

Moses, then, lived on without visible memorial to help people's memories, just as he would (we feel) have wished. He was 'the servant of the LORD' (Deut. 34:5), specifically the prophet beyond compare (v. 10) and the continuing repository of the word of God to the people of God (v. 9). Once a lady said about her departing minister, 'I don't know what we will do without Mr .... He used to explain the Bible to us.' Every true Christian minister will echo that epitaph with, 'Oh, that it might be said of me!' Every true Christian believer will long for the same reputation of solid devotion to the word of God.

Divine grace will make us like Moses in other respects. Like him we too will come to the day and moment of death 'as the LORD had said' (v. 5; literally, 'by the mouth of the Lord'). There is no such thing as an untimely death (cf. 2 Kgs. 2:1–3; 1 Thes. 4:14, which literally reads, 'those who have fallen asleep through Jesus'). Moses died, not through failure of natural vitality (v. 7) but because the Lord said so. We too have the eternal privilege of being known by God (Gal. 4:9). Indeed is it not remarkable that Moses' epitaph does not say he knew God – which he did! – but that God knew him (Deut. 34:10; cf. Matt. 25:12).

Devotion to the word of God, while it is a thing in which divine grace will surely be magnificently and actively on our side, calls for commitment, determination, the discipline of constant reading and the hard graft of memorisation. This is what it means for us to be servants of the Lord; this is certainly what it means if we are to be prophets of the Lord, ministering his word to our generation.

REFLECTION

Take heed: the Bible begins with humans adding to the word of God (Gen. 3:3) and then disobeying it (Gen. 3:6); the Bible ends with warnings against adding to or subtracting from what has been revealed (Rev. 22:18–19).

REFERENCES

1 Henry A. Collins, *'Jesus, my God, my Lord, my all'*.

2 Nahum Tate and Nicholas Brady, *'Through all the changing seasons of life'*.

3 Author unknown.

4 Charles Wesley, *'Jesus, we thus obey'*.

5 Edward H. Bickersteth, Jr., *'Peace, perfect peace'*.

6 William D. Longstaff, *'Take time to be holy'*.

7 William Walsham How, *'O Word of God incarnate'*.

8 P.P. Bliss, *'Hallelujah! What a saviour!'*.

Alec Motyer
DEUTERONOMY
AT JOURNEY'S END
44 UNDATED DEVOTIONS THROUGH THE BOOK OF DEUTERONOMY